"A poem," says Nancy Dunham at the start of this lovely collection, "is like a road that lets us travel / farther than the way we've gone before." Reading these poems, her journey becomes our own, where "who we were becomes a moment in the passing, / and who we are becomes the place we want to go." The dream-like quality of the author's lines can be truly mesmerizing, and her descriptions are often breathtaking: "I see a bird above me, / wings spread wide and holding on to air / like swimmers in the lake might hold on to water." Dunham's Ohio landscape includes jazz clubs and nuclear power plants; fruit trees and train tracks; the ever-present, enduring lake; and at least one mirrored bar room where "everything about the room is an illusion, / and everything about the room is real."

She teaches us to ride the dolphin's back, to enter the mind of a faithful dog, that we might purchase the shiny gold box found in a jewelry store without ever thinking to question what's inside it. This debut collection, so charmingly illustrated by the author, is deft and beautiful, testament to what rises from the unconscious when we allow it to take the reins.

—Paula J. Lambert, author of *How to See the World* and *The Sudden Seduction of Gravity*.

Inside the Flow
Poetry

Nancy Dunham

Bird Dog Publishing
Huron, Ohio

Copyright © 2021 by Bird Dog Press
All rights reserved.
This book, or parts thereof, may not be reproduced in any
form without permission from the publisher; exceptions
are made for brief excerpts used in published reviews.
ISBN 978-1-947504-28-8
Bird Dog Publishing
PO Box 425, Huron, OH 44839
Lsmithdog@aol.com
http://smithdocs.net

CREDITS:
General Editor: Larry Smith
Cover & Layout Design: Susanna Sharp-Schwacke
Cover Image and Interior Images: Nancy Dunham

ACKNOWLEDGEMENTS

To my love and life-long partner, Richard, who has kept us safe and strong these many years.

The encouragement and suggestions from others have helped me bring this collection into being. Many thanks to Richard Norgard, Patrick O'Keefe, Kurt Landefeld, Larry Smith and other friends at Firelands Writing Center for their invaluable support.

Table of Contents

Introduction 7

Preamble

Poet's Domain 11
Jar of Marbles 12
Winter Solstice 13
Door 14

Part One: Landscapes

Three Musings on a Latent Spring 19
Jazz at Slater's 21
Room of Candlelight and Flame 23
Post Office 24
Early Friday Morning in Port Clinton, 1989 26

Part Two: Destinations

Italian Elegy 31
Prayer 34
Robert Frost 35
There are No Walls in My Imagination 37
Jungle Cat 38
Dolphin 40
My Dog Jim 42
Kaufman's in Bowling Green 44
The Cherry Tree 46

Part Three: Rites of Passage

Moonwalk 51
Moonlight ....,.. 52
Breath and Indian Summer on Lake Erie 53

About the Author 59

Introduction

Nancy Dunham tells us why poetry matters in the first lines of "Poet's Domain."

> To walk with poetry is to have a dream
> so clear and satisfying, it takes us where
> we might not ever think we'd go—confection
> from a mix of air and breathing,
> and there it is, a moment that is true.

Dunham's poems draw readers into that confection, a world of images in search of meaning. Images stack upon one another in quick succession, all somehow connecting to reveal a truth, a truth the poet requires. Her truth is not a complex philosophy nor a simplistic religious credo but resides in nature, people, places, experiences, and so these poems remind us where to look for meaning in our own lives.

Seeming tapped directly from the poet's subconsciousness, this first collection from Dunham is lyrical, sensual, dreamlike, creating collages of ordinary things. She layers details, employs sensory cues, to build a representation of this human journey, each layer its own revelation, in a dovetail or juxtapose to find its own reason. The results can border on the surreal, but we are pulled along by a credible, authentic voice, and the life described we find familiar.

Using the first person and the collective you to good effect, Dunham creates an intimacy that engages the reader. We share in a childhood memory ("The Cherry Tree"), find a solitary moment in a moody jazz club and enjoy a walk in a small town on a fine morning, knowing the names of people and places, feeling at home, belonging.

Other poems skirt modern worries. In a dream she is haunted by a letter she wants to mail ("Post Office"). Who is it to? What does it say? The questions within the poem make us feel uneasy, so much is unknown yet seems important. In "Three Musings on a Latent Spring" the specter of the Davis Bessie nuclear plant looms over Lake Erie. But the underlying anxiety of these poems is time, a life ticking.

Dunham longs "to be taken into the arms of something greater" ("Breathing") and her lyricism shines in poems that move seamlessly between reality and fantasy. In "Dolphin" the dead and *bloody eyes* lead into the wonder of being swept into the sea. The shapeshifting exhilaration of "Jungle Cat" is particularly sensual and fantastical. She slips in and out of animal personae, opining at last, "I don't know if I am going but . . . // If I do, I won't be coming back."

Dunham is a spiritual nomad recording what she encounters along the way, trusting that something important may be revealed. She contemplates more questions than answers where the important questions rarely have ready answers. Yet we sense the writer is comfortable inside her flow. The zone. A mental state of total immersion. Being fully in the moment. Ready for the truth. What a wonderful head space for a poet.

The voice inside the flow of these poems is comfortable with the truth of a good life. And so, in "Indian Summer on the Shoreline of Lake Erie" when the poet bids us . . .*take a final breath and call it harvest,* we understand it at a cellular level. We have only the moment now, but it holds all the moments of a lifetime.

—Connie Willett Everett is a writer and editor.
She is publisher of *Pudding Magazine*.

Preamble

Poetry's Domain

To walk with poetry is to have a dream
so clear and satisfying, it takes us where
we might never think we'd go—confection
from a mix of air and breathing—
and there it is, a moment that is true.

To learn to break away from moments that divide us
and hold on to the kind of sense that lets us see.
I think if only we could always have it
there wouldn't be a world that causes pain.

In each of us there is a way of being,
the same as what is true for someone else—
to dream that we are part of something broader—
it is always there and waiting, when we try.

A poem is like a road that lets us travel
farther than the way we've gone before.
It is always there and when we find it,
it might be like a bluebird flying by,

It might be like a fountain in the sunlight,
it might be like the thunder from the rain.

I want to write a poem that tells a story
of what is real and true for everyone
living in this world all together, yet
at the same time, how it feels to be alone.

Jar of Marbles

I am looking for you in the blue green shimmer
underneath a cloud. Oh, let me in,
where color lives inside a jar of marbles,
a secret like a genie on a shelf.

Reach inside and pick another color
that is looking for a way to reach outside
like a day that's clear and you are walking through it,
something strange and different at your feet
.
You feel the rain like hands that tap your shoulder.
You're not in the dress you wore the day before.
You are marching to the music in the distance.
You are running down a field in your sleep.

The football stands are loud and full of people,
jumping up and yelling for the team.
I see two rows away where you are sitting.
You turn around. You look straight back at me.

I knew your name but now I have forgotten,
only that your hair blew brown across your face,
and the night was there with what we knew we wanted,
even though our school lost the game.

They tore the goal posts down, but I remember—
magic was the moonlight in your eyes,
and who we were those days across the city,
riding home from school in the yellow bus—

boys you thought of in your bed when you were sleeping,
colored dreams like marbles in a jar.

Winter Solstice

Take a walk across a field in winter.
The sky above the trees turns creamy purple
where a patch of snow has left a pale path,
and out beyond the trees there are the houses—
one street at a time and there you are,
a set of railroad tracks to cross
or look far down into the future.
There might be cities there or riverboats
and maybe someone in the shadows waiting
or maybe someone standing by the bridge.
And who we were becomes a moment in the passing,
and who we are becomes the place we want to go.

Door

I face a door.
The frame around the door is from an oak tree
that once grew somewhere else,
a hill or in a garden,
or even on the outskirts of a woods.

The life behind the polished grain
is lost or hidden in planks that hold
a wooden door in place. The planks
are smooth and quietly recessive
and fits within the colors of a room.

Although the door is closed and hard to open,
I feel the spirit of its worthy will,
as if it were a wish or something living
on the other side, another life.

A field full of weeds, a winding river,
a hunting party and the fox who slips away,
the roads that rise and fall like floating ribbons,
reaching out like fingers on a hand.

And are they fingers from the hands that build the bridges,
or sew the dresses that a city girl might wear?
Will I meet her one day if I am walking
down a sidewalk where a street musician lives?

The street is lined with doors and little porches
and every porch is open to a door
I am standing outside of and knocking.
Someone on the other side is looking back.

I might stay and yet I want to keep on searching.
for in a house, my father said, are many rooms.
Some are merely rooms with empty spaces.
Some have open windows, chairs and desks.

Some are parts that live in my imagination.
Some are parts that live nowhere at all.
Put them all together in a package.
Roll them out like dice across a lawn.

Warm as snow, warm rain, warm taste of coffee
dripping from the edges of the cup.
It is like a place that's there without a reason—
it's like another life without a door.

I am in a rowboat floating on a river.
The pieces of my past are going by.
I might want to, but I know I won't go out there.
I wave them on, and at the same time, call them back.

I am standing on the threshold of a moment.
The life that presses up against me is a door.
The day is there if only I will take it,
pull it up like an umbrella, walk around.

A penny for a piece of candy in the window,
a dollar buys a ticket for the show.
There are birds with great black wings that fly above me.
There is sparkle on the surface of a pond.

There is the fox, I think he wants to find me
and snuggle up his nose against my lap.
There is the sunlight coming through the window.
There is the touch of fingers on the knob.

I step outside—I leave the room behind me.
I saddle up my horse and ride away.

and after that I think there might be music,
and after that I think there might be love.

Part One: Landscapes

Three Musings on a Latent Spring

1.

Looking up I see a bird above me,
wings spread wide and holding on to air
like swimmers in the lake might hold on to water,
air-fresh each time I take another breath,
another breath that takes me where I'm going—
I walk my song in footsteps on the ground.
The earth becomes the air that I am breathing
I feel the wind around me flying by.
Neither down- trodden nor at the same time soaring,
I am just a woman with a pencil in her hand.

2.

Dark sky. "We are heading into rain," my husband tells me.
The sky looks dark above the distant trees.
We are driving east toward Port Clinton and Sandusky—
Behind us lie the edges of a town.
The car is moving with the speed of light,
and somewhere up ahead it must be raining.
I think of water coming from the sky
as if someone turned an ocean over on us,
and we are fish and time is going by.
We take the turn around the curve at Bono,
Davis-Besse waiting up ahead,
and where is God if not around this curve?
Different clouds, a road that keeps on going—
I am here and closing in on eighty.
Not much time left to think about the sky.

3.

Davis-Besse is a great gray concave silence,
imposed like a stranger on a friendly shore.
Nothing like it in the space around it—
a strip of land where grasses used to grow—
a shoreline where the water swirls between the limestone,
the wind makes sounds that rustle through the leaves.
The cooling tower is made of blocks of concrete
that take the space of what was there before.
The secret is the making of its deepness.
You can see the rising steam from miles away.

Jazz at Slater's

The long slow note is how it feels sometimes,
outside the door of Slater's in Port Clinton
where I go because I like to hear the jazz
that's slow and slanting in the falling twilight
with what is coming from inside the horn.
Wet breath the way the sound picks up
and drifts out down the sidewalk, to where
the lake spreads wide on summer nights.

Back down the street, I walk in from
the sidewalk, not in darkness,
more with a sense that overtakes me
when I feel a rhythm deep inside my bones.

He wears a derby hat, the trombone player;
the music that he plays is slow and sweet
inside the room, but what I notice
is the figure of the singer who is standing
in the open space beside her by the bar.

I haven't had a thing to eat since morning.
I feel it now, the hunger in my soul.
I sit down at a table next to John and Peggy,
Paul and Garret on the other side.

My eyes become accustomed to the darkness.
I don't want to talk. I pass off a smile
and turn toward the bar so I can see her,
Anna Givens who has picked up the rhythm
coming from the center of the horn.
She is singing, a quick spray of her voice
that matches tempo. She is weaving

in and out of melody and a call to anyone
who wants to listen. A slow, strong
kiss of music makes a ripple,
the tremble of the singer calling back,
calling to a world that will let her
be whoever she becomes inside the song.

The tempo travels on. It doesn't mean
to stay locked up forever. It breaks out
now like birds across the sky,
up and out like someone tossed a flower,
inviting each of us to be with her.

I look at Anna and let her take me with her,
as far as anyone knows how to go,
all settled in the satin she is wearing
and nothing but the inside sound of jazz.

Room of Candlelight and Flame

Candlelight on faces of the people
reflections in the mirrors on the wall.
Oh, Mr. Magic, Mr. Storymaker,
let the candle be the light behind the eyes.
We sit like cats waiting underneath the table,
snatch a bit of food and run away.
Then comes a little music from the bandstand.
Someone rises from the table, starts to dance,
and now the shadow-motion is the dancing,
and everybody in the place is taking hands,
and what happens now is not a story
or a piece of shadow from another dream,
but you are there beside me. You are talking.
You tell me all the things I want to hear.
I want to stay but now the dance is over.
You put a piece of candy in my hand.
It's time to go. The candy has a taste of
something tart and biting, from an apple tree
that's growing outside in our yard.

Your fingers on a keyboard ruffle water.
The wind along the shoreline plays a song.
I am young again and outside washing windows.
I squeeze the rag out tight and wipe the glass.

Post Office

I was standing on the corner when it happened.
I was just about to walk across the street.
I had to come across a bridge to get here
The river is a passage and connection
that makes a little stream into the lake.

The street behind me lies in shards of broken pieces,
the footsteps one by one that brought me here.
Footsteps from the places I have come from
leave a path of moonlight trailing back.
I like the road that runs along the river,

I like the way it feels, wanting more,
Sometimes there are places on a highway,
traffic moving in and out of time.

A letter is a way to make connection
when a mailbox is waiting, miles away,
to find the one to come along and say
I'm glad I found you, open up the letter,
read the words.

But for a brief delay I would have been here
gone up the steps in front and through the door.
Footsteps tap across the marble surface,
a woman sitting on a stool behind a wall..
I need some stamps. She asks for twenty dollars.
I think I hear some voices in the back,

a long walk down the dim and narrow hallway,
a slit of pale light beneath a door,
a radio, a pot of coffee, people working.
No one told them it was time to go.

Did you ever get a chance to read my letter,
or did it vanish when the wind began to blow?
I have walked a block from Maple Street and Perry
I found a place where I could leave my car.
Darkness now has swallowed up the edges
and left me here alone beneath the trees.
The lights are gone from spaces that were windows
or did I only think that's what they were?

Across the street, I hope the door will open,
someone coming down the concrete steps.
And what is it I think I must have wanted,
standing there beneath the trees at night?

One block away, between the bank and drugstore,
a single light that hangs above the street—
reminds me there are times I need to put together
what is not forgotten with the new.
I have this letter in my hand I have written.
I need to get it in the mail by tonight.

Early Friday Morning in Port Clinton, 1989

The old man sitting on the bench along the sidewalk,
a sailor's cap is slanted on his head.
He holds a pipe, yet doesn't smoke it.
The pipe is like a flower in his hand.
Down the street the blossom shop is open.
Mary parked her car and went inside.
Early Friday morning in Port Clinton,
sunlight on the sidewalk from the east.
Let's go to where the walk becomes an alley,
slipping back behind the fronts of stores.
The awning yet to be unfolded on the gift shop,
a dog is sitting on the step beside the bank.
A car is edging toward the traffic light on Second,
train wheels turning on the tracks above the street.
Underwoods is open now for breakfast,
and Adelaide is walking down the block,
her long skirt swinging back and forth across her body.

A line between the darkness and the daylight
tells me it's time to start another day.
I cross the street, the jewelry store is open
I remember that I have to fix my watch.
Little boxes sit out across on the counter.
Mr. Kleinhans needs to put them all away.

"Good morning, Mrs. Dunham, can I help you?"
"Open up this box," I say, "I'd like to see inside."
The box is gold outside and has a
satin ripple that shimmers like the waters by the shore,
and if I asked Mr Kleinhans, could I buy it,
he'd answer, "don't you want to know
what's there inside the box?"

"I like the box," I say, and "yes, I'll take it."
I put it in my purse and walk away.
The sun is shining out across the water.
On Perry Street, the cars move back and forth.

Part Two: Destinations

Italian Elegy

1.

A train is rolling through the open country,
slick between the wind on either side
It passes by so quick you hardly notice,
the long low shapes that move across the landscapes
like separate moments in a single life.
A woman in a window that is passing
bends an arm and looks out through the glass.
You wonder how it would be, there beside her,
sitting on the seat inside the train.

Someone walking by the door of her compartment,
the smell of coffee drifting through a hallway,
she can slip out into, any time she wants to,
walk the aisle front to back in shaky feet.
And now it is the thought that you are going
somewhere you have never been before—

Did you ever ride a valley in the darkness,
turn up the radio and let the music take you
anywhere the music wants to go?
We were young and we were there together.
We were in a car and riding through the hills.
We were on a road that faded off into distance,
with scattered lights like someone sprinkled stars.

And now inside this train where I am riding
I can see the light inside the car ahead.
The porter with a tray is bending over
a child who's sitting in the seat below.
It is close inside the place where I am standing.
Did I hear a voice that called my name?

2.

The train has come into a little station.
I wasn't sure what I was doing there.
The platform by the train was wide and open.
There were little shops that lay on either side.
A young man in a red cap loads some luggage
on a cart that he is pushing through a crowd.

I heard it once, I know it must have happened.
I saw it once and wished it wasn't true—
a whooooosh of air so sudden I could feel it,
cool like a draft against my skin.
Not wind, more like a force that were it earthly,
would turn the world around me upside down.
I had a dream the night before I lost you.
It wasn't anything we talked about.
We put our clothes into a leather suitcase.
It was hot in Italy that time of year.
We drove up to a little village in the mountains.
We stopped along the road because we wanted coffee,
and there it was across the field, the wedding party.
The bride wore a poppy in her long dark hair.

Her father stood around a little table
pouring amber wine into a glass.
The sun is shining low behind the mountain.
The field was full of blossoms on a hill.
You bought an apple from the little grocery.
You ate it, walking back toward the car.
On the backseat shelf your socks were drying.
You started up the car. We drove away.
The road along the mountain ridge was high and winding.
The world was like another hill to cross.
And what we thought was all about tomorrow,
was something lost we could have done today.

We were heading down a causeway when it happened.
There wasn't any way of going back.

Prayer

Let there always be a flower
just beyond me,
roots like threads
that weave a warm
place in the dirt,
maybe going all the way to China
I used to say before I knew where China was.
If only it could
be there in a field,
white and wild and tiny in the grass
where we were children once
and walked
knee-high in clover,
the smell of earth and what is there beyond—
the boulevard that turns into a driveway,
Beechway on to Copeland and the River Road.
There were places I could go to pick a flower,
hollyhocks that grew against a wall,
petals like a blossom on a toothpick,
a bud you put on top to make the doll.
And if I call out to you in the morning
will you find me where I
went to dream last night?
Brown weeds, long tongues of grass, a field of poppies,
a place where flowers grew before they died.
It isn't that I have to go and find you.

It's only that I have to know you're there.

Robert Frost

You taught me how to feel the rocky coastline,
your pencil on the edge of earth and land
like hay out in the field before you cut it,
plowing up the ground behind the horse.

Spring in the air. The vacant lot is waiting.
You might have left the plough and slipped away
to sit beneath the apple blossoms in the orchard,
to smell the scent of spring and try to hold it
there in words that write a day into a poem.
I read to my students from a textbook,
two roads diverging in a yellow wood.
to sit down on a log or swing with birches,
to let the feel of it take us on.

You plant a seed in spring, it grows in summer.
It finds a way to last until the fall,
and if I found you underneath a tree and you were sleeping,
would you say hello and let me in your dream?
I hear the pounding of the ocean on the shoreline,
I feel the difference in the mix of fire and ice,
and if I knocked upon the barn door, would I find you
sitting late at night beside a lamp?
A little light falls there across your paper
and all you want to do is write a poem.

The sickle slants the words toward a harvest,
a neighbor's fence becomes a secret song.
A little hour of time before it passes—
you write it down before you go to sleep,
the way a poet's dream can last forever,
like footprints left behind you in the snow.
The way you reconcile the world of other people—

good fences make good neighbors, so you say.
And if I asked you as a poet, would you tell me
what it means to live with fire and ice?

If I would tap your arm and ask you, would you take me
down the path where way leads on to way
and if there is another woods beyond me,
how many miles would I have to go?
Well, you say, it's all in how you ask the question,
somewhere ages hence and with a sigh.
Hard edges up against a poet's yearning—
you have to hold your ground, to draw some lines.

It's true, you said good fences make good neighbors,
but something else that doesn't love a wall.
And that's all fine, I say, but I don't think you've answered
what it would take to learn to write a poem.
You looked at me a long time before you answered.
I thought I saw a twinkle in your eye.

Oh, Robert dear, I love your earthy wisdom
caught in between a lyric and the line
the curve of life held up against a moment—
you put it all together in a rhyme.

There are No Walls in My Imagination

There are no walls in my imagination.
There are no barriers to hold me in.
There is another world that lives inside me,
rearranged from anywhere I've been.
It isn't always something that is pretty,
it isn't always something that is good.
It's more as if there is a spirit waiting
for a mind and will that it can call its own.
So who is it, friend or foe that might be waiting,
mind and will that lives inside me now
to tell me how to put a life together
in a different way than how I've done before.
I crawl into my bed, pull up the covers.
put on my magic cape and go to sleep.
And take me to another kind of freedom,
take me to another kind of land.

Jungle Cat

Falling like a feather through the silence,
floating like a ribbon in the rain,
sunlight, swinging in between my footsteps,
cat eyes peering from around a tree.

I see myself reflected in the shadows,
moving slowly through the purple jungle grass.
Beneath my feet is yet another cushion,
paw down on a place between the leaves.
I listen to the chatter of a birdsong
halfway up the hollow of a tree.
I don't look up. It is
enough, I tell myself,
to be here, careful how the moment makes me feel.

I don't remember how it was I got here.
It seems like I've been walking all my life.

Up ahead and down a path there is a clearing
and a feeling that I want to try again
from inside out, the other side of living,
raindrops on the underside of leaves,
and nothing but the sweetness in the burning
of the campfire in the clearing up ahead.

Do they need me anywhere that I'm not going?
I don't think so. Do they care? What does it matter
if they do? Do I really want to stay like this forever,
prowling through the space between the trees?

I'll not be afraid of cat eyes that are watching
or spirit birds above that call my name.
There is a place ahead and now I see them
huddled close like birds inside a flock,
and if they come out looking, will they find me?
Could I still slip back to where I was before?

The ferns are feathered high where I am watching
and wet enough for me to feel the cold.
I put my ear close to the earth to hear the pounding
of hoof beats running fast across the plains.
And now I want to be there running with them,
hot sun above and burning on my back.

We are moving now, the horses all together.
I slap my hand across a sweaty flank.
I lean against its neck and feel the breathing,
the rise and falling of the gallop as we go,
the warriors close enough for me to touch them,
their lips and eyes are lined with purple paint.
I don't know yet if I am really going,
but I'm thinking, maybe,
and if I do, I won't be coming back.

Dolphin

The dolphin on the beach had bloody eyes
and spots along the edges of the mouth.
It seemed to pull me closer when I saw it,
the way its shape lay helpless on the sand,
the water lapping up in little splashes
reaching out like hands that pull away.

Hot sun and people on the beach were running forward
like those who might be bearing witness to a crime.
What the dolphin might have been before it happened,
what was once, and what might be again.
And I was there, and I was swimming with the dolphin,
holding with my arm around his shiny back.
The tail like a rudder cutting surface,
he let me drift and roll among the waves.

He took me to his places in the ocean.
We passed through rising weeds like tangled sand,
and once he looked at me and spoke of time and trouble
and said somehow it wasn't like that here,
and in his eye I thought there was more kindness
than I had seen among the others on the shore.

He could move us by the shifting of his body—
just a little turn and we'd be on our way.
I let my hair string out long behind me.
I felt the ocean press against my skin.
I didn't breathe. I found I didn't have to.
I was moving with the current and the tide,
up and down like riding through the rapids
or quiet in the presence of a kiss,
and once upon a time he let me ride him.
He let me climb upon his slippery back,

lean a little to one side and let the billows
hoist me up to where I found an easy stride.
I wrapped my legs around the arc that was his body
and on the ride the water splashed up high,
and on the ride, the sky became the water
so free and fresh I'm never going back.

My Dog Jim

There they sit as though they don't even see me
and all I want to do is be there with them,
my master and my mistress—
Do they really care what all those others have to say?

I want to lie down close beside my master,
sit up on his lap so he can pet me,
tell me what a super dog I am.
She does too, kind of. She gives me supper when I want it
pets me when I climb up on her lap, but really,
there is, with him, a steady kind of comfort,
and I can feel it deep inside,
for I am smart for a dog, and they know it.

I am responsible. I always tell them when I have to go outside.
I sniff beneath the leaves until the place is right.
I can tell by the scent that rises from the grasses
as though some other dog had been there first.
They wait for me. Good dog, they say
when I am in the car again beside them.

This new place we live is not like home
but all that matters is that they will take me with them
where they go out or when it's bedtime.

I want that now and I try to tell them.
Don't you know you have to
get rid of all these people?
Listen to me now, I try to tell them.
I don't care how you do it, but it's time.

I didn't mind so much when I was younger.
I could walk into the kitchen, get a drink.
I could go outside and chase the squirrel
who was always waiting for me
It would streak across the yard for me to chase,
running just as fast as I could go. ZOOM!
I'd be close behind. I'd almost have it,
but it would always leap to safety just in time.
No matter. I will wait. I will lie in the grass
until I see it peak at me around the center of a tree.
Haughty squirrel. He gives his tail a flick as if to taunt me.

It makes me so mad. I jump around beneath the tree and bark.
I tell him I'll be back to get it, and when I do
I'll shake it silly, then I'll kiss it
and let him loose so he can run again.
I dream of chasing squirrels and when I'm sleeping
sometimes I hear them calling in my dreams.
Jimmy, Jimmy, they call in squeaky voices.
I know that squirrel knows that I'll be back.

In the meantime, I need to let them know that I am waiting
for it' getting late and time to go to bed.

Kaufman's in Bowling Green

The neon from the street outside the window
blends with the fading light beyond the sky.
We are sitting in a booth inside of Kaufman's
after class downtown one day in Bowling Green.

Black Russians have the taste of coffee,
sweet with alcohol. I take a sip.
Sandy is sitting there across the table,
scarf dripping wet for it is getting cold.
We have come here this afternoon to wait for David,
but David won't be joining us today.

The waitress comes and Connie gets tequila,
and there are people sitting at the bar—
the old professor who remembers David,
and said to wait for him, that he would be here.
The sounds inside the room begin to blend together,
the way a moment overlaps a word.
We are sitting here at 4 p.m. at Kaufman's.

There isn't any way that David will be back.

And now the warmth I feel inside has started working,
the way the flowing words can come and go
and let another world come to life inside us.
David was the one who tried to show us
how it felt to be the one to write the poem
and read them, sunny afternoons inside the student union,
sitting there together after class.

It's getting late and Sandy still is talking.
She is making up what she forgot to say.
The room is like an empty world of people
who see themselves in mirrors by the bar
and everything about the room is an illusion,
and everything about the room is real.
It's too late now but still I dial up his number.
I watch the door and wait for him to come.

Cherry Tree

I hadn't thought about the cherry tree for years, the
way the bark made shiny creases in the sunlight and
how the limbs thinned out in narrow branches and in
those notches where I placed my feet. A kind of
haven off the ground that I could go to, as if it spread
out above the whole neighborhood, and I could see through
the stucco, around the corner of the house and down the
street, sweet and airy when the cherry blossoms
bloomed in spring, pink for just the time it took to
grow a leaf.

To learn to climb the tree and how I did it, holding on
to the first limb with my arms, then swinging up. I'd
find a branch to slip my foot into, like a stirrup, then
swings my body up and into place. I put my arm
around the trunk to lift up one notch higher, the tree
tall going up but getting smaller, looking down.

There is the fence that closes in the backyard and a
place where the ground makes a little dip. I always
wondered how it got to be there, that strip of earth
across the yard that lifted up. Did someone make it
be that way on purpose, or was it just a little whim of
God who dumped it there to be a challenge that made
it hard for me to cut the grass?

The back yard is a place with grass beside a gravel
driveway and the gate they closed to keep our dog
from running free, the way that life could be part of a
single vision, the way it felt to be a little girl.

There was a Christmas tree my father planted close to
where the garage and back yard met. I didn't think it

ought to be there, but who was I to say I didn't like it,
the way its limbs drooped and feathered soft in
little branches, not stiff and green like other Christmas
trees. The house was stucco and the roof came to a
peak and then it slanted down into the backyard
where the cherry tree was growing, almost like a poem
the poet wrote.

> *"Up into the cherry tree*
> *who should climb but little me.*
> *I held the trunk with both my hands*
>   *and looked abroad to foreign lands."*

Sometimes I liked the view that I was seeing, but
there were other times when Mrs Kell, the next door
neighbor, sat on her back porch, two eyes peering up
between the branches, two eyes that did not belong
with this great smile of the morning light upon me,
the light that shifted through the pattern in the leaves.
It was my life, was it not? to climb any tree I wanted
without permission, and if I slipped way up there high
and slid a bit and had to grab on to something, well, it
wasn't anything for Mrs. Kell to see, and if I got lost
somewhere in the years that turned like pages, it was
only story after story like trains that roared along the
backtracks, folding little moments into dreams.

People were astonished, so my parents told me, when
they thought a child was reading, sitting on a bench
somewhere in public places, Robert Louis Stevenson's
book in my lap. I knew all the words by heart that lay
beside the pictures. My parents read poems to me
every night. Mother Goose lived in that large boot of
the old woman and what it meant to live your life
inside a shoe. It worried me a little, all those children
running in my lap loose across the pages, and did I

really know those other people out there who were watching, surprised to think a little girl could read?

Flame inside the fireplace on Medford Drive in winter. Smoke that licked its yellow tongue across an evening, words that traveled with me came around each year as just another story. You could see it in a movie, you could read it as a chapter in a book. You could taste it like the sour juice of cherries when you got enough to put them in a pie, when you came down from the tree and went in the back door to the kitchen, my mother cooking something on the stove.

I never thought of where I might go after that.

Part Three: Rites of Passage

MOONWALK

A sliver of a moon is a single hand that beckons
from a cradle rocking high above the trees.
Soft sand from a road that runs beside me
on a path that narrows slowly into stars,
lifts me up to how it feels, watching God.

There are things along the way I haven't found yet
like spirits rising slowly through the mist,
my father in a little fishing boat out on the water
and nothing else but echoes on the waves.

Green hands of trees are clinging to the wetness,
the leaves that hold you to another day.
I want to walk at night along the shoreline,
to be at one with what is waiting there.

It's not that darkness opens up my thinking
with footprints left behind that no one sees,
but out beyond is something like a lantern
swinging back and forth across the waves.
It tells me there are secrets in the making
for what is more than I know how to say.
Let it be all right to listen in the morning
for what I left behind me in the night.

Moonlight

Full shadow from the moonlight high above me,
and silver outline on the edge of passing time—
I wander through the street around the villas.

I can only guess at what I wouldn't find.
When you dream you search inside a story
for love and life that hasn't happened yet.
Imagine you are standing by a river.
There is a path of ripples from the moon.
You let the river take you on a journey,
dark downstream as far as you can see.
The wind behind you creeping through a meadow,
a feline body moving through the grass.
You take your hand and drop it in the water.
The water, as it swirls around your finger,
leaves a silver trail floating back.
It doesn't matter now where you are going.
The moonlight on the water finds the way.

Breath and Indian Summer on Lake Erie

There would be no kind of life without the breathing,
air cold against the skin or warm as day,
I breathe. I let the air go deep inside me.
It passes through me like a breeze of quiet wind.

I take a breath of air and hold it for a moment,
let the breath move slowly in and out.
I feel the air, how it holds my life in balance.
It settles in my brain and in my blood.
I take a walk because the day is sunny,
or go outside to breathe the autumn air.
My footsteps touch the ground where I am walking,
I breathe the moment as I walk along.
What miracle to have the air around me—
as if the world is passing in and out.

To be taken into arms of something greater,
than who I am when I am here alone.
The weather is its own determination.

It is its own device for when to change.

I feel no weight, no sense of stepping over,
out from one landscape into something new
that goes as far as I can feel it, warm in sunlight,
humid in the tropics of the mind.
I take a walk across a field in winter,
white and clean and knee deep in snow.
I ride my bike along the street in summer.
The air is soft and I don't need a coat.
I am sliding down a hill toward the river.
I let my hands float high above my head.
I wear a skirt. I feel the wind is blowing.

It brushes on my arms and on my hair
I am a child again and I can feel it,
the fingers of the air, the endless time.

Across the lake I see the waves are rolling—
great gulps of breath that rise and sweep away.
Breathe in, breathe out. I let the backwash lift me
up into a cresting of another wave.

I breathe it in, the fresh air from the water.
I breathe it out, like waves inside my bones.
I feel the endless rhythm in the lapping,
a universe that's breathing in and out.

Indian Summer on the Shorelines of Lake Erie.
I am coming from a meeting at the club house,
the room so noisy that I couldn't think.
The sky tonight provides a grateful silence.
Outside of me, the darkness IS the night.
The darkness spreads out high above the rooftops.
I lift my eyes and look toward the sky.

Dark circle of a shadow moon against the darkness,
a silver light that shines around the edge.
The language of the moonlight draws me forward
like hope that helps me start another day—
and everything I know is all around me,
and everything I know is what I see.

When you dream, you find yourself inside a story.
You let the darkness tell you where to go.

By September what is left of summer will be over.
By October look out through the colored leaves.
You hear the geese, the dying of a season,
you see the birds are flying overhead.

You see the sun. It sparkles on the water
as little lips of waves explode with light.

Breathe in, breathe out like rhythms on the water,
the motion and the lapping of the waves.
Breathe in, breathe out, the air is getting cooler,
the final days of what was here before.
We take a final breath and call it harvest.
Put on your coat. It's almost time to go.

About the Author

Nancy Dunham taught English for 25 years at Port Clinton High School in a community on Lake Erie about an hour from Toledo. Her greatest interest was with creative writing and the arts. Nancy grew up in Toledo and attended Ohio State for two years after high school, graduating from the University of Toledo with a Liberal Arts Degree.

Besides literature and writing, she also taught classes in the visual arts. In 1977 she completed a Master of Fine Arts degree with an emphasis in Creative Writing at Bowling Green State University. In addition to enhancing her craft, the program was an opportunity for valuable new friendships and increased awareness of the importance of good writing in our lives.

As a teacher, Nancy took great interest in her students' skills in literature and writing, which took shape in student writing competitions, a school creative writing publication and a writing club. She was a reviewer for *Ohioana Quarterly* and served as the nonfiction editor of *The Heartlands Today*. Nancy is a long-standing participant at the Firelands Writing Center, where she continues to engage in workshops and public reading opportunities for personal growth as well as community interactions with the arts.

She and husband Richard are the parents of three children, Mark, Suzannah, and Theo. She and her husband live along the shores of Lake Erie in Port Clinton, Ohio.

Other Books by Bird Dog Publishing

Lost and Found in Alaska by Joel D. Rudinger, 242 pgs. $18
Mingo Town & Memories by Larry Smith, 96 pgs. $15
Trophy Kill by R. J. Norgard, 256 pgs. $16
Symphonia Judaica: Jewish Symphony and Other Poems
by Joel D. Rudinger, 117 pgs. $16
Words Walk: Poems by Ronald M. Ruble, 168 pgs. $16
Homegoing by Michael Olin-Hitt, 180 pgs. $16
A Wonderful Stupid Man: Stories by Allen Frost, 190 pgs. $16
A Poetic Journey, Poems by Robert A. Reynolds, 86 pgs. $16
Dogs and Other Poems by Paul Piper, 80 pgs. $15
The Mermaid Translation by Allen Frost, 140 pgs. $15
Heart Murmurs: Poems by John Vanek, 120 pgs. $15
Home Recordings: Tales and Poems by Allen Frost, $14
A Life in Poems by William C. Wright, $10
Faces and Voices: Tales by Larry Smith, 136 pgs. $14
Second Story Woman: A Memoir of Second Chances
by Carole Calladine, 226 pgs. $15
256 Zones of Gray: Poems by Rob Smith, 80 pgs. $14
Another Life: Collected Poems by Allen Frost, 176 pgs. $14
Winter Apples: Poems by Paul S. Piper, 88 pgs. $14
Lake Effect: Poems by Laura Treacy Bentley, 108 pgs. $14
Depression Days on an Appalachian Farm: Poems
by Robert L. Tener, 80 pgs. $14
*120 Charles Street, The Village: Journals & Other Writings
1949-1950* by Holly Beye, 240 pgs. $15

Bird Dog Press
A division of Bottom Dog Press, Inc.

Order Online at:
http://smithdocs.net/BirdDogy/BirdDogPage.html

www.ingramcontent.com/pod-product-compliance
Lightning Source LLC
Chambersburg PA
CBHW021000090426
42736CB00010B/1398